JUVENALIA

JUVENALIA

Poems by

Reid McGrath

Cover design by Shay Culligan

ISBN: 978-1-950462-51-3

Kelsay Books Inc.

kelsaybooks.com

502 S 1040 E, A119
American Fork, Utah 84003

For Elaina

"I have drunk ale from the Country of the Young,
And weep because I know all things now."

—William Butler Yeats—

"Young knucklehead: Today you'll bruise your thumb
To harden you to pains to come;
The sun will burn; the heat will cause you sweat;
Dust will choke before the sun is set."

—Michael Curtis—

Acknowledgments

Some of the poems herein, whether online or in print, have appeared in the following publications: *First Things, Trinacria, The Society of Classical Poets, The Lyric,* and *The Epoch Times.* The author thanks the editors of these publications, especially Mr. Evan Mantyk. He also thanks his family for their undeviating support and inspiration.

Contents

After Getting Off the Bus

For my parents

(In Response to Timothy's Steele's "Practice")

No more could frogs or tree-forts entertain;
I hadn't started track at twelve-years old.
The thought of doing homework was insane.
I'd find the ball where yesterday it rolled.
I'd huck my bag onto the fresh-cut lawn
á la Achilles sloughing shield for sport.
I'd schmooze the dog who'd cry then idly yawn;
tighten my shoes and hie out to the court.

Manipulating lineups in my mind
I'd play the parts of all the All-Star stars—
A flash of Briseis, bright-haired, bleachered, blind
to my air balls—The driveway filled with cars.
Such introverted solitude was choice,
but so was your rote, dinner-doling voice.

The Backwards Romantic

"Most of those once common occasions for poetry seem embarrassingly old fashioned now that piped-in tunes and hand-held devices provide the background music for life's journey,"
—Dana Gioia

I'm prone to loathe the radio and television, noise
from all angles, laptops, Ipads, cell-phones—
the gibber-jabber of the wired boys
and girls. I crave the silence of the Stones
of Venice, eerie quiet, sacred sound
that's not quite sound: the wind-chime's plaintive tune,
the creaking trees in snow, a shrieking loon
on a morning lake where fog and calm abound…
I'd have preferred a horse-cart out tonight:
with only the yotes yipping and the clop
clop-clottering of horses—by the light
of lantern—who knew when and where to stop
without a map, much less a GPS.
Endangered Silence causes me distress.

Ars Poetica

"Make it new,"
  —Ezra Pound

"I think we are in rat's alley
Where the dead men lost their bones,"
                    —T.S. Eliot

I too have known your yard of scattered bones.
I'm tired of your rows that no one hoes.
I like to keep my affairs in order:
to walk, through strange cities, like a soldier.

So let us go out now to rat's alley
and clean up the stacked pile of debris:
of old and naily and forgotten wood,
engulfed in burdock, pokeweed, but still good,

beneath the barn-bridge where a cat sits still:
prepared to pounce, to swat, and then to kill…
There's a snake skin; there's some barbéd wire!
Behind the tank there is a tractor tire!

And we will go and we will build something
that has some form, that took some tinkering.
It will be "new" just like a snowflake is,
how every orchid's different from all orchises.

Without trying to be something it's not,
a bluet blooms amidst the woodland rot.
It'll be as symmetrical as it can be
to frame the chaos of our history.

The Formation of Rock

Pressure is what the dirt feels when, buried
and dis-tracted, it cannot function right;
when it cannot access the rain and light;
when it, by a hellish heat, is harried.

When it is not prepared, or preparing,
to produce, what it was meant to produce;
when its physical makeup is not loose;
when it's sick and tired of temporizing.

For what it wants is to produce good fruit;
to rise like cream out of that sub-terrain.
But who we are is never absolute;
and via all the pressure and the pain,
solidified like some rare earth-bound loot,
it settles by becoming rock again.

The Dare*devil* Within

One mountain goat traversed a precipice…
I thought about how close we live our lives:
two double-lines away from the abyss,
one drink too many or two nodding eyes.
The young live in a cloud of nonchalance,
a heady high the old often condemn.
And yet some saints displayed insouciance
when persecutors persecuted them.

My confidence would get its gas from faith
and works — to have a moral certainty—
that when the ground gave out my contrite wraith
would join the angels in eternity…
I watched the goat traverse a precipice,
while I was still adventuring on thin ice.

A Vocation Condoned

I wandered by St. Joseph's Church—
(The old one where they had the school.)
Up in the belfry pigeons perched.
On asphalt tepid puddles pooled.

The rhododendron's leaves were dull
against the lattice aged with moss.
Out in the baseball field I mulled
upon my landlocked albatross.

The shingles hung—as by a thread.
So did the hoops from off the rims.
With cynicism lost or dead,
I craved another pseudonym.

*

I know that church was just a church;
and yet I hear dead priests that sit
like ghostly rockers on that porch
calling to me—the hypocrite.

I still am haunted by that place.
The doors all locked. The look inside.
I saw a dusty holy trace
of something halcyon that died.

The vibes were restive in that church
and all is restive in my soul.
I left it largely in the lurch
without a bell to tug or toll.

Juxtaposition

Here is a blonde-marked maple tree:
stands by the road so stolidly
while mourners make their floral shrines
and in the night a taper shines;
but soon the taper will burn out
and yet the tree will remain stout;
and it will stand for years to come
spreading its leaves beneath the sun.
and in the Fall will drop them too
and with some Springs its bark renew.

Us mourners, we, will go to bed;
but where can a tree lay its head?
It does not budge or cringe or cry;
and does not ask the question: "Why?"
It's just another token man
is done in by his own élan.

What He and Michelangelo Know

"There on the scaffolding reclines Michael Angelo,"
—Yeats

The Hudson's sunk in this great vale of blue.
The Catskill's hackle bristles in the sky.
The setting sun transforms the clouds into
earthlike layers that Time does stratify.
This is no Rome, nor would I wish it be;
this is no dome that demigods do paint.
This is a whitish shed under a tree;
and the man painting it is not a saint.

The soffit is a place that's hard to reach;
so I stretched out my hand to brush the trim,
funambulist-forethoughtful lest I reach
too far and fall into the Obscure Dim.
Thus this, at least, we have in common now:
I've felt the paint that's burned me 'neath the brow.

Reconnaissance Missions

Some agent or some spy on foreign turf,
      I've traipsed the City specter-like, alone.
On Coney Island I paced off the surf
      and futilely assayed to skip a stone.
I too have walked down darkened urban streets
      and felt how I've felt in the Northern woods
with busted compass, when the light retreats;
      when either fear, or plucky resolve, floods.

I've played the covert poet on the greens.
      In Central Park I sought a daffodil.
But a park's ends will never match its means:
      It tries to imitate a nonpareil.

      My heart has pledged allegiance to the land;
      I've *liked* the City but it's built on sand.

My Lake District

This lake has not always been so lonely.
These hills behind it: not always so brown.
I begin to think of friends and family:
Fires, manhunt, cycling around the town;
I think of pickerel caught when we were five;
I think of relatives no longer here.
I sit by this blustery lake and revive
fond memories of love, health, and good-cheer.

I have been so fortunate and lucky
and yet I've taken it for granted, I
have screwed so much up, neglected to see
the value of other people. We die
on our own; and aloneness has undone
this Prodigal, finding no one home, Son.

Lines Composed Before Finding "The Society of Classical Poets"

Savants like to arrange their stars
and push their poets into piles:
marble-misers who assign the jars
according to the artists' styles.
They line them in their fusty den
when they deem an era's past,
and deign to burp them now and then,
but work to invent a 'new' cast.

Classicists have since ceased to be,
and Rhyme is out of fashion now,
but She still moves me like the sea
rocks a sun-soaked splintered scow.
All good men have come from men,
like oaks which out the leafmeal sprout;
what once was old appears again:
It is an everlasting fount.

Sportsmanship

"Writing free verse is like playing tennis with the net down,"
—Robert Frost

When he was young he cheated like a dog.
He was ambitious and a smidgen vain.
He wanted to compete as if the god
of coaching need not call his golden name.
Like other cheaters, he made up the rules.
If "Man was God" then he'd make something "new."
He thought the bench was for losers and fools
who'd never win a 1st Place ribbon: blue.
He played alone on lineless, netless courts.
He always 'won;' but, hey, what do you know?
He ultimately saw this wasn't sport,
but shirking putting time in—O no no!
You've got to ride the bench and learn the law
before they cheer your number and Hoorah.

Men Before Work

for Dana Gioia

It's dark and cold. The fleet comes filtering in.
They take a breath. They get out of their cars.
Half-hidden in a cowl-like hood, their heads
are bent like friars walking through the fields.
Their coffee cups are hallowed in their hands.
The balmy vapors defrost the frozen air.
Some smoke, hung over, and the younger smile,
while jaded old ones pace like beasts in zoos.

The boss approaches like a quarterback
knowing the call, with bacon, egg, and cheese.
Directions given, the huddle's broken up.
They fling their lunch-filled satchels in the trucks,
make some remark about an irksome wife,
or steep in saintly silence till they're there…

Self-Imposed Exile

I stood in the back
at the Poetry Reading.
"Do you write?" she asked.

If your right hand writes
let not your left hand know. "No."

Epiphanic Hangover

I wake up with cruel cotton-mouth, a head
that feels like an old attic without air,
with creaking floors and spider-webs. I said
I'd never drink again. I've got nowhere.
My body's like an unoiled machine.
A dreadful fear and apprehension haunts
my schizophrenic conscience. Was I mean
to those I love? How did I answer taunts?
With fists to face? (My hand is sore.) I rise
to get some needed water from the sink.
It only will get worse and I'll despise
myself all day, spent in surviving. Drink
has always wrecked me. The first step, they say,
is admitting that you are not O.K.

The Modern Cynic

Distrusting, thus starving, with an ungrateful suspicion,
he murmurs at his Moses in his Wilderness of Sin.

Irish Haiku

He called his Guinness
a blonde girl in a black dress.
They were good for you.

In the Galway Bay,
old people in blue swim caps
swam. It was snowing.

In Connemara,
parked, and no one on the road.
I smelt the starving.

They called Limerick
"Stab City." "My sister lives
there." "Sorry," they frowned.

The Dawn Sleep

My anxious soul has bothered me all night.
I lie awake without Sleep's soothing balm
which relieves stress; I toss and turn; I light
a candle by which I can live a psalm.
My hypos get the best of me, I fear
a death alone in a black static night;
and even when I start to nod I tear
my eyes back open lest I should alight
in that black void. I spend a night like this
when like a mother creeping up the stairs
slowly and softly, catching unawares
my nervous spirit dwelling on black Dis,
she lightens the sky, tames my morbid mares,
and with her lilac lips my eyelids kiss.

*Hypos: short for hypochondria; allusion to the first page of *Moby Dick*

*Dis: the abode of the dead, the underworld

The Holistic Physician

You know the boons of contemplation, thought,
ardent study, reading and reflection;
you know that the mind and the soul will rot
deprived of prayer and meditation.
Our bodily frames also deserve respect:
as tabernacles built of bone and flesh;
as vehicles and temples which affect
our soul's demeanor and keep our thoughts fresh.
If mental illness starts within the gut,*
then Diet's vital to our sanity;
and Exercise, which cleans residual soot,
burns Diet's fuel which promotes energy
and fosters Sleep. So quit your study. Go
learn mens sana in corpore sano.

*Hippocrates

35

Retreating Snow

Like an old man dragging his long white hair
out of the lawn, back toward the forest's shade,
the snow retreats, cornered, and well-aware
of time that's up and warmth it can't evade…

Young blonde Apollo bays this crumbling foe
and inch by inch reclaims the tawny grass;
and while there is a time for fresh-white snow,
one does exclaim: "At last! At last! At last!"

His Palomino team touch on the ground
and pull their pony-cart over the fields
spreading their burlap-color all around.
Tan Phoebus*, with his long-bow that he wields,
steals back the landscape, conquers the old snow,
which—soon enough—will have nowhere to go.

*another name for Apollo, the Greek sun god.

Spring Haiku

I'm optimistic:
like a brand new tennis ball,
everything's chartreuse.

The brook-trout's belly
is like a sunset I saw;
its stipples the stars.

Papa bears hungry.
He tests his weight on the bough.
I'll need more birdseed.

The dog running laps
round the yard for no reason
is how I feel now.

Stopping by Courts on a Sunny Morning

for Robert Frost

One night-crawler out on this sparkling court,
dried-up and shriveled, overdone, not red,
neglected to take heed, or to report
'twas all mirage; to turn around instead.
Followers, these, in the benighted hours,
had wriggled out to nab a bit of wet;
who in the sun wilt faster than flowers.
This holocaust is something to regret.

If one was living: I was curious.
I paced the court off with an eagle eye.
The cocky sun was sure, was luminous.
But near the fringe happily did I espy
one writhe (or throe); his pain would I allay:
I threw him in the woods and went away.

Rushing to Get the Hay In

I. The Farmer's Wife

He may as well be sitting on a piece
of junk john-boat out on some open lake.
The field is shorn, divested of its fleece;
the hay is tedded and the rusty rake
is resting now beside the tree-lined wall
next to the tedder, stilly looking on,
like two quaint collies waiting for a call;
while there, in wagon, stacking, is my son.

While there, cat-black, looms a portentous cloud,
white-veined with light, or crackled, like a glass;
and there, my husband, donkey, that's too proud,
endangers himself and my son, alas.
But then again if we don't have the hay:
we probably won't last winter anyway.

II. The Farmer

Oh press on honey we are almost there.
Most faithful tractor that I've ever owned.
Pulling a baler that pulls up the hair
of Mother Earth which she has kindly loaned;
which we in turn will feed to hungry kine,
and store in mow where dust shines down in slants;
and feed it out right through the wintertime.
The cows will spread it like some active ants.
I am not worried; I believe in you.
No rain will touch our sun-dried, fragrant hay.
My wife's a wart who doesn't have a clue.
No lightning will touch down on us today.
My son, too busy, cannot count the gap
between the lightning and the thunder's rap.

III. The Farmer's Son

I cannot think; it's sad; I haven't time.
The bales come quick the quicker that he goes.
My hands are creased and cut from the harsh twine.
We bounce along over the humpbacked rows.
I bounce and lurch and blist with hands quite numb,
the field like some flag striped without the stars,
my body baked and broiled by the sun,
we war with Nature yet we love these wars.

Lo and behold I see the dark thing too
out of the corner of my mote-fraught eye.
I cannot look and yet I know the blue
is flagging to the black that's coming nigh.
As long as I'm his son: I cannot quit;
no matter if, with lightning bolt, we're hit.

Indolence; or, a Dude on Vacation

With last night's fun like fog within his head,
on sunny deck, encased in house's lee,
Franklin's *Autobiography* he read—
or tried to read, over his black coffee,
but laid down on the toast-warm wood instead.

The Lunch-Break

for Carol and Tuck

He sat upon a hard, foam-rotted seat;
the leaves were glittering in the torrid heat.
He knew that it would be a special feat

to go much longer without drink or food;
when out the dusty blue his girlfriend stood,
with cucumber tomato sandwich good,

a can of cold which beaded in the sun.
His first break since the haying had begun;
and he knew that she had to be the one.

Sturnus vulgaris

A starling's like a waif who isn't coached,
some spoiled brat who mimics in retort
right after (by you) he has been reproached.
He got the gun out for a little sport.
The starlings are the worst, and he would pot
them all, if he could; oh the way they shriek!
He bird-proofed his garage; he'd kid you not
to get back in it, took them just a week.
But starlings, too, are like those gopher things
at carnivals who go back in their hole
before you pound their brains in and it stings
(all the worse) your red and ornery soul.
Of course, right when he had reposed his gun,
the vexing menace shrieked by towards the sun.

Blue and Yellow Barn-Swallows

She made a note to note when they arrived.
It's obvious whenever they finally do.
Over the cows they dipped and ducked and dived:
"They have two houses; shouldn't we have two?
I wonder where they stay in Mexico?
Or maybe Florida? Or some Texas barn?
Either way, darling, we will never know;
and here they are again: stealing the yarn!"
Adobe nests, clinging to white-washed beams
festooned in spider-webs, were tidied up
by swallows who came flying through the seams
of wood, or glassless windows, where they'd sup
their chicklings on regurgitated gnats,
deftly, and agile, like diurnal bats…

The Little Vector

A Ten-nos*

My knee is like a cantaloupe: I am a humbled man.
It seems brutal that you are a part of the Master Plan.
The Desert States have scorpions; the South has rattlesnakes;
Australia and hot Africa have beasts within their brakes.
The Sea has sharks, the North has grizz, Islands have weird
spiders;
while those in Northern Asia have Siberian tigers.
The Amazon has piranhas and the black caiman too.
Here in the Hudson Valley we are mostly plagued by you.
Because you're small, you are a threat; your bite won't even prick.
If left unchecked: your Lyme could kill. You are a bloody Tick!

**A ten-nos, the word sonnet written backwards, is a poem of ten lines (five couplets) of iambic heptameter created by Bruce Dale Wise. A sonnet is frequently 14 lines of 10 syllables; a ten-nos is 10 lines of 14 syllables.*

At the Buffalo Farm on Long Island

Of course—to plains—they're largely unaware.
They've only known a barn, a concrete pad,
this patch of dirt which at least flaunts fresh air.
They don't know what their ancestors had had.

They look at me. The poor bastards. A dearth
of wild joy or romping life exudes
from out their eyes. Ten acres of this earth
and not a single blade of grass protrudes.

These hooves were meant to stampede wolves and men,
to stamp indentions into fertile sward.
Rainwater would combine with seeds therein.
Regrowth conferred next month's replete reward.

But now their hooves are grossly overgrown.
They're curled due to their sedentary ways.
Their lot's compacted. Cobs bestrew the loam.
The whole place reeks of general malaise.

Summer Haiku

On Dutcher Golf Course:
7 irons at 7:00.
Locals play for free.

They say her beauty
was like rockets in air. We
jumped off cliffs in Kent.

I live in Pawling
with "Robins' egg" porch ceilings,
horses and split-rail.

The best ice-cream shoppes
are yellow; Heinchon's abides.
The Help doesn't hurt.

Drinking a Beer and Watching the Fireworks over the Village of Pawling

George Washington—on Purgatory Hill—
Feted his men to beer and barbeque.
On this same slope—loafing in laurel still—
I peer out at the pyrotechnic view.

America

A red bandanna and blue jeans—
One Rand McNally atlas—
War monuments on village greens—
Driving the kids to practice.

The Greenhorn, Up in the Air

Up in the air: clamoring cloud; and twenty-one—
I go out looking for the Country of the Young.

The light turns green. I feel the green rain with my hand.
I walk to where the green mountains meet the white sand.

I read too much Rimbaud: "Where do the lime-trees grow?"
Now I'm back in green woods; yet I crave the white snow!

Up in the air: tempests twirl round; and twenty-one—
The rip-tide pulls me to the Country of the Young.

And so coming in daggers the green neon lights
illuminate the puddles with greens and with whites.

I reach for the laurel; yet I grab the white air.
I'm greenly rebellious; I don't want to be square.

But then the storm wanes and the greenest sky turns blue.
I learn to love temperance and I turn twenty-two.

Lamenting Our Complicity in the Installation
of Suicide Nets

I met a "bum" outside an Apple store
holding a sign which read: "I'm taking bets."
"On what?" I said. "On something that'd abhor
maybe the most insensate, calloused vets."
I curiously said to tell me more.
He had no problem, being garrulous:
"In China, in the dorms, the employees
will jump the window to forget the fuss
of toiling with iPhones—O the bane
of treating people like robotic bees!
I bet that, from now on, you won't forget
the pain resultant from another's gain.
You will envision a suicide net
and you'll shop different cause we're all to blame."

On Super Bowl LI

I went to bed. The Falcon's made it 28 to 3
and yet I never should have doubted the poised Tom Brady.
Halfway through the third-quarter he had a ways to go.
I woke up in the AM and was quite flummoxed to know
the "Comeback Kid" achieved what's now the greatest comeback
in
the history of Super Bowls: "The first overtime win!"
He was an underdog at first back in 2002.
A gamer, clutch, cool as a cuke, wearing red, white, and blue.
Now Alpha Dog, his successes provoke large love or hate;
but either way, with "damns" or "ahs," one must admit he's Great.

Lines Composed in the Adirondack Mountains

The sap is glommed up on the fragrant pines.
I savor the air as I take a walk
around the lake, admiring the signs
brown and yellow, forgetting how to talk.
The coffee's perked when I return; I stoke
my friend the wood-stove. Outside blooms the smoke.

Lines Composed upon the Mid-Hudson Bridge

Changeable is this river while I drive
over this bridge with pylons that denote
which lanes are eastbound, which are westbound; I've
looked down upon these cheeks of ice which float
upon the water's surface like a face
that changes its expression every day.
The tug-boat ploughs a furrow black; its pace
is like that of the turtle's, towards the bay;
Another day the river is a map
with continents, tectonic plates, that shift
in thawing warmth when trees let-down their sap,
or like the squares of fieldscape when you lift
off of the runway, in a plane. I love
the Hudson, in the winter, from above.

Observations both Literal and Inferred on
The Course of Empire by Thomas Cole

I. The Savage State

The foreground is dark, sublime, and savage.
Storm-clouds roll up towards the right; the ledge
reflects the setting or the rising sun.
The turquoise waters crash; the storm's not done.
One bounding buck leaps over a green creek.
One brutal hunter, chiseled like a Greek
stone statue of a herculean man
wields a long-bow in his outstretched left hand.
There're tee-pees and a fire on the right:
a semblance of domestic warmth and light
in this savage, Paleolithic state,
wild and rough and rugged, if irate.
Adam, out of Eden, with all his kin,
who Cole paints as a white-skinned Indian.

II. The Pastoral or Arcadian State

Like the storm, Cain's gone, that murderous rover.
The land is cleared. Trees are felled. The clover
and grass (that terrestrial plankton) grow
naturally, unlike the crops we sow.
The rain, the sun, the fertile loam nurtures
this Neolithic town's verdant pastures.
They raise white sheep. White togas women wear.
One man is plowing with an ox. The air
is post-storm fresh. An old man pokes at dirt
sagaciously while Holy Fire's girt
by a Doric, crude-columned-thing atop
the plateau where the tee-pees were. They stop
their running over land: They build some boats
as leisure, love, and calm seas raise their hopes.

III. The Consummation of Empire

Pastoral simplicity—for Classical
complex white structures—'s doffed. Symmetrical
domes gilded with gold and marble lambent,
Corinthian columns—Caesar planned it.
It's glowing whitely. It is beautiful:
The ferns in urns. Doubtless reputable
drapers who sell the sails and fabric pink,
peachy, purple, and soft like silk, I think
are rich. They all are. There is a statue.
The bay is like a mirror. The sky is blue.
The fountain signifies outpouring wealth.
But the staid rock seems leery of their health:
their excess leisure which turns into sloth,
lust, gluttony. Their mouths begin to froth.

IV. Destruction

It's not Sublime; it's Death; it's Terrible.
It's the augured Sickness transmittable
because of myriad sins rife in this world.
Greed, pride, envy, wrath are all here unfurled,
as barbarians in Viking-like ships
storm and raid and plunder. Red fire rips
through Caesar's City while the sable smoke
billows up toward the leaden sky. The yoke
of slavery is imminent for those
who aren't raped and drowned. The indisposed
take their own lives, jumping into the sea.
The rock still means: Immutability,
when juxtaposed with temporal mankind
who winds itself up only to unwind.

V. Desolation

Then it's over. It's evening. The doves hoot
from the sagebrush, tangled thickets, then scoot
with iridescent necks up to some spot
where they now nest amidst the marble's rot.
The air breathes well. The Romantic ruins
are consumed by ivy, moss. Some bruins
come down from the high hills and roll the stones
of ancient relics looking for old bones
to gnaw on, grubs, or leftover honey,
not caring one whit for all the money
bestrewn upon the dirt. The placid sea
reflects the moonshine. This is how it'll be
when the Flood ebbs, when Life respawns again.
Dame Nature is a swift custodian.

Knowing How to Lose

(Honesty is a thing that's hard to brook
when you are with one who is too honest,
and who is working not at your behest;
who without words, but with a telltale look,

turns in an instant love to jealous hate,
because their heart pines for another's nest,
and in your arms they couldn't find their rest,
and learning of it you become irate...)

With her intrigue she pulled upon his strings,
washed his body, with perfumed soaps galore;
some great hero, who washed up on her shore,
only to wrench apart her hopes of rings.

If all he wanted was to be set free,
She could do it; she could bear it, she swore...
If all he wanted was the sea; implore
Her for it and she would vouchsafe it he.

But it was not all of travel's allure
that he wanted: the adventurous life.
Nor Achaeans, though he thought of their strife
nostalgically, proud but always demure.

It was not, ever, the immortal way.
"Ah, goddess," he said, "you are not my wife."
and hearing it, Calypso, she was rife
with defeat, and sent him home to Lopé.

Three Trojan Perspectives

for E.E. Club Saw Reid

I. Priam, Returning to the Ramparts

He'd never say it to my face and yet
I sense that Hector senses I'm washed up:
too old, too soft. Not that he is the pup
that sees for the first time his dad beset
with something he can't handle, can't repair—
No, that was long ago; I feel ancient.
I'm sick of war and I am impatient
for things to go back to the way they were…
Think of Agamemnon, Odysseus,
dexterous Diomedes, jacked Ajax,
AWOL Achilles, and Menelaus—
By Zeus! Who could watch? Paris is too lax,
Trojans all. The Achaean army'd be a dream
if only they had Hector on their team.

II. Paris, Back in His Bedroom

Because he never let me fight my fights—
too protective, he always interfered,
having an older brother's heart, he jeered
at me in private, but on public nights
painting Troy red, when we were fun and young,
and when some badger mocked or called me out,
I never even had the chance to shout
before big Hector, Priam's favorite son,
had pushed me back, and got into the face
of that poor fool—I've got a lover's soul,
 not a fighter's. They call me a disgrace!
 loathe me like Black Death, whereas he is "cool."
I know it all too well that I've been spoiled.
Helen smells this coward who's recoiled.

III. Hector, in Front of His Men, Kicking at the Dirt

It's ridiculous all the times he's quailed:
say when we'd got to wrestling round the shocks
of grain (for fun) or on the salty docks
of some sea-town where we, as kids, had sailed;
and where the local thugs, reeking of fish,
would test our guts when chaperons let us be.
He's never had the right integrity;
and off he'd flit before they served a dish
of knuckled fist smushed in his pretty face.
He is a chicken whereas Menelaus
is like some redbone barking at the base
of a tall tree. My brother is a wuss,
who I thought changed, but again let me down.
Especially cause Troy is our hometown.

Fathers and Son

I. The Modern Daedalus

I want you to carry yourself with pride:
Stand up straight, with your shoulders back; don't slouch;
and yet, also, don't let hubris deride
you. Be humble. Get off that cushy couch
I only could afford by working hard,
from the ground up. Now come into my shop.
We'll woodwork, weld; go out into the yard:
You'll get a dead-car running, hear it pop.
Shake hands firm; the respect of men you'll earn.
Paint with care, clean your brushes in the sink.
Help me plumb, solder, shingle the roof, learn
to like learning: Math, Science, etc.. Think
for yourself; but know you don't know it all.
Otherwise, son, eventually you'll fall.

II. The Modern Icarus

I need to do it my way. I am proud
of him, a lot; he's like a Superdad.
He's so well-rounded; skills in him abound
which none of my buddies' fathers have had.
And yet, what is it about his shadow
that makes me want to rise up above it?
Is it a son thing? a human thing? Go
higher, faster, farther; I don't love it.
It's capitalistic: beating one's dad.
It's stupidly progressive; it's insane;
and yet it's in me. I have got it bad.
This social instinct or my pride must wane.
For when he tells me to slow down or die,
some perverse imp decides I ought to fly.

The New Proteus (a New York version)

"I either wear really nice suits, or I look homeless,"
—Mathew Konchan

You've probably seen him in Manhattan suave
dressed in a suit that's dapper, with spruce shoes,
a slick coiffure and fluent. What's improv
to versatile men? So now peruse
his résumé. It's lengthy. The next day
out in the Sound with Suffolk fishermen
who wrangle ropes and slur, come home and pray
in a wind-whipped church, kneeling, there he is.

You'll see him in Museums; he likes Art.
You'll see him milking cows and mucking stalls
deep in the Catskills, far from men, he'll dart;
then yet again exchange his coveralls.
He plays all games; he Adirondack shoots.
He makes an argument that he refutes.

Creativity Craves a Cave (an Apology for Form and Rhyme)

Imagine Gretzky "trapped" behind the crease;
or Pelé, deking, swarmed before the net;
Odysseus before he dons the fleece;
or Jordan, bodied, ere he stops to set...
It's in tight spaces, when one is constrained,
when one is challenged, tangled, forced to find
a resolution or a route that's aimed
forward and not down a path that's blind,
that one can get the best out of oneself:
creating pathways theretofore unknown.
Rhyme and form are good in and of themselves,
if not for Song, then also as a cone—
some pylon that we dip around, contrive
so that in some End-Zone we might arrive.

Offensive Defense; or, Watching a Guy Play Ping-Pong

Most of his offense is steady defense.
He spins the ball; he grins; he's lightly taxed.
Methodical, stoic, surreptitious,
he's out for blood and yet he looks relaxed.
Life is largely a battle of attrition:
he returns all that his opponent smacks
(with too much fury) in his direction.
Consistently defending—he attacks
his foe's composure: gets beneath his skin.
He keeps his form while his foe sloppily spikes.
Whoever makes the least mistakes will win.
This type of play not everybody likes.
He doesn't showboat, serve it super-fast.
His greatest talent is that he can last.

On the Morning of the Terrorist Attacks
in Brussels

I've tucked my upright thumb back in my hand;
I have decamped and taken down my tents,
and now stand restive on the secure sand
while you are sailing in the elements.
I wonder if you're safe. We never were
brothers who called or used technology,
to check in or to chat. I still prefer
to let those live who live their own story.
And yet I'm worried. I know that you're strong.
And yet I know geography too well
to know that Delft's not far from Brussel's throng.
And just outside of Heaven there is Hell.
Thus here I am on this suburban beach
praying your waves are temperate with this speech.

View from the Wallkill Valley (a tanka)

Like a submarine:
gray flanks and conning-tower—
or Leviathan—
rising out of the water—
the rugged Shawangunks crest.

Laurel Blossoms

They are exotic
and simple at the same time.
That is elegance.

Summer Dreams

Before the full brunt of the night had settled
the warm smoke slithered like a snake on the grass.
I was sitting at a table of metal,
which held a pencil, a book, and a cold glass.

After the gazebo: a lucent blue pool,
surrounded by gray cement, and then a green sward;
behind that a garden, and therein a gnome on a stool,
who, while I drowsed, 'mongst the dewy flowers, became a bard.

The Cherry Orchard

I. Trying to Find a Presence in the Cherry Orchard

I strolled between the cherry-trees and felt a presence there.
I was intoxicated by the sweet, perfuméd air.
I was alone and wandering but heard across the path
of dandelioned, verdant grass an innocent young laugh.
I pictured a cute artsy girl with camera round her neck
but couldn't see her for the pink of blossoms: What the heck?
I tried to take a shortcut and cut in between the rows
but God had put up obstacles and that is how life goes.
I glimpsed her in the pink of trees, against the azure sky.
I had to catch her. Yes I did. I couldn't say goodbye.

II. The Presence in the Cherry Orchard

She strolled between the cherry-trees with camera round her neck.
This hobby had distracted her from ugly Life's black wreck.
She loved the pink of blossoms and the yellow dandelions.
Upon her tan young shoulder was the constellation 'rion's.
She kissed the petals like a bee; she breathed their sweet perfume.
She took a picture she'd forget but someday would exhume.
She walked upon the grassy path compressed vaguely by tires,
and while she walked the angels strummed upon their golden lyres
up in the cerulean sky with feathery clouds of white,
not knowing that one day she'd be my own euphoric light.

Valentine

I didn't know when Valentine's Day was,
and didn't need to. That day came and went
like any other. Now I know it cause
you're perfect, dear; you don't know what you've meant
to me, my life, completely ignorant
to Love which waters a lush Happiness,
as if my rose-like heart were pinched and pent
up in my dry yet sunless parchéd chest.

You have refreshed; you irrigate my heart.
You're water and you're sunshine and you're air
that's unpolluted: cool then warm. You part
the darkness of my isolated lair.
Now fertile is my chest; and a Love grows,
and now you are my Heart; you are my Rose.

Marriage as a Dance

Everything that's living craves Existence:
Plants stretch for soil, sun and sky, and rain.
What creature will not devise a defense
against destruction and impending pain?
Of entities with constituent parts,
like ecosystems—engines which burn fuel—
my heart is one. But in my heart of hearts
you are ensconced like an illumined jewel.
More potent than petroleum or wine,
I crave your fuel that helps my engine run.
Beatrice led Dante nearer to the Son
as you help me back to my Maker's manse—
Who is Existence; He designed the dance
and called it "Good." His ducks were in a line.

Fall Haiku

New England college
towns: Pumpkins, apples, breakfast
in a warm café.

Like a robin's breast:
rusty colored barns, silos
draped in bittersweet.

In their black pea-coats,
off of the Metro North, the
leaf-peepers arrive.

Cross-country, small-town
football, the leaf-smell hunting—
God I love the Fall...

Memento Mori at the Lakehouse

I don't need skull or hourglass to muse
on looming Death or fleeting Time. I have
the sober afternoons when all our friends
and family return to their normal lives.

It's then we're left along after we've cleaned
the lake house up, the Adirondack chairs,
which once circled the fireplace. The trash
is put out front; and no one's on the lake.

We thought about this weekend for a year;
and now it's gone. We stand upon the shore
my arm around your waist. The sun will set
with no one watching and the stars will shine.

I always need to have a goodbye beer.
The Guest Book's signed. The key returns to post.
We pull into the road and drive away
while half an earthworm shrivels on a hook.

Tares in the Wheat

"No man, having put his hand to the plough, and looking back, is fit for the
kingdom of God,"

Luke 9:62

When I recall various seeds I've sown
I'm prone to clench my teeth and tug my hair.
I look back on the lea and it looks bare.
My bag of seed was by the devil blown
chock-full of tares, not wheat, misleading plants:
Green at first but browning on the easel.
I'm upset; but relieved that it's legal
to change my name, or move, or to supplant,
to start afresh and bury the old crap,
is comforting. I keep my eyes ahead,
on the offing, tighten the safety strap,
and press on plowing till I'm spent and dead.
The juvenile weeds were a mishap.
From now on (try!) I'll make Prudence my friend.

The Untrue Artist

"The true artist will let his wife starve, his children go barefoot, his mother
drudge for his living at seventy, sooner than work at anything but his art,"
—George Bernard Shaw

I've put untapped potential on a shelf
much like a book one someday wants to read.
I'm less concerned with cultivating "Self;"
and now am more concerned with what we need.

We're married. You're more beautiful than books.
The Muse is not my mistress anymore.
Despite how mainstream or mundane he looks,
the Pragmatist is no one to abhor.

If I can make it to retirement,
I'll pen the poems you deserve to hear.
But if the artist in his art is pent,
I'll eschew those poor penthouses, my dear.

I hope you know that when I stoke the stove,
get out the door, then labor out of sight,
I show my love—not with poems of love,
but with books of poems I won't write.

Adaptations

If Romeo Had Received the Letter
(An Alternative Ending)

Part I

Romeo (in the catacomb, lying down beside Juliet)

The friar's note said "Romeo she will wake."
Thus here I am now with my life at stake.
You'll resurrect? Or will the potion err?
the anesthesia taken on a dare,
a hope that it will work, won't stop your brain;
I start to think that this is all insane.
You are my other half; I'm facing you.
Our eyes, like wounds, one inch apart. Into
your mouth, your nose, I breath. I crawl; I turn
beneath the pall, not facing you. Discern
my back now 'gainst your back. I feel you move!
Aristophanes "whole-human" would approve.
A caterpillar in this sick cocoon;
I'll wait to morph out of this backwards spoon.

Juliet (One month later. She is sitting at a plain wooden table with
a few crumbs on it, a dirty plate and glass, a vase full of wilted
flowers, with some flies in the tepid and murky water. Romeo, who
is gazing absentmindedly out of the window into one of Mantua's
more sordid city streets, has two empty wineskins of Cabernet
Sauvignon in front of him. The apartment is small and unfurnished
and you can hear the mice in the walls.)

So here we are in Mantua. What now?
Where once was sun a darkness clouds your brow.
You stay inside all day in this bare flat.

We don't have money; yet you're growing fat…
Tell me how that works, Romeo? Recall
our honeymoon, how ripped you were, the hall
we ran through, to our rooms, shedding our clothes.
We really made love everywhere: God knows
we sinned; we did; but not in that way, no,
we were married; but Moses said: "I show
you these Commandments blazed into this rock
'Obey your parents. V.'" Is it a shock
we suffer now financially, are shunned?
The friar's plan was fry-ered; I just punned.

Romeo

Our honeymoon is done. There is no dough.
We went to where the honeymooners go:
to Rome and then to Ischia where the hares
are raised in pits, and fished out, sat in chairs
out in the yellow sun at some cafe
consuming bread and cheese and wine all day,
prosciutto from an acorn-finished pig;
I clenched in purple teeth an English cig.
We laid in bed all day, or by a pool,
or on the beach, or on the balc'. The cool
sweet air, from off the water, blew the sash.
We burned and burned through bonfires of cash.
For one month, oh; oh, what a life we led?
But now that month is gone. Our love is dead.

Juliet

What were we really thinking? How could we
leave all our fam behind? Just you and me?
It sounded nice while in that catacomb
but Verona's the place I call my home.
It is the place that you call your home too
and that is why you hate me, why you're blue.
Our dreams were dashed against slipp'ry rocks!
Our dreams, like cars, should come with built in shocks
to mitigate the jolt of when they crash,
because of speed and speedbumps ere they smash,
careening towards the cliffs of Life, the sea
of what we know is mere Reality…
We should have got to know each other first.
The play goes poorly when it's not rehearsed.

Romeo

You say I'm growing fat; I'm growing old.
A young man ages quick pining for gold.
I don't know what to do; I've killed my friends
by getting in the middle. Make amends?
with who? O you Mercutio are dead
who always mocked those silly books I read:
Petrarch's sad numbers, Dante's early work
La Vita Nuova. I was wont to shirk
my duties for my father, Montague,
my studies in the classroom: "O boohoo!"
I wailed against my fate. My fate was good!
It's just that I had never understood
the maxim bout the fishes in the sea.
You were, I thought, the only girl for me!

84

Juliet

I should have put you through more tests—my fault.
I was bombarded by your strong assault
of passion, ardor, language; Paris too
was knocking at my vestal door. I flew
into that bone-crib, drank the vile up,
for you, alas, the better looking pup,
the better talker, poet—Pilgrim, ah
and here we are exiles in Mantua...
O Romeo, I'm sorry, you're not bad;
it's just that when I think of what we had,
I think that life is one complex mean trick.
The gymnast needs to be coached ere she stick
her landing safely on the padded mat.
My kinsmen hate me; I blame me for that.

Romeo (after a minute, growing visibly contemplative and
remorseful)

You sound like Helen. It is not your fault.
I was the Trojan Paris. I assault
you even now, when I should go to work,
get off my ass: The breadwinner can't shirk
the onus that he owes to his nice wife.
The problem though is my entire life
I haven't worked at all; nor have I said
I'm sorry, when I should have. O we're wed
we might as well get on with it; I'm changed.
What if our marriage wasn't pre-arranged?
Perhaps you didn't love me like you thought;
you're blameless, girl, two Parises had fought
for your white hand. I had the better tongue.
Should we go out tonight? I'm feeling young.

85

Juliet

We'll take a walk. I want to talk tonight.
I am so glad we do not have to fight
about this any longer. When they see
us working on our marriage. It will be
clearer to them that we have settled down;
we have matured, are serious. The clown
of our old love has lost its squeaky nose.
Call our old love: "Pinocchio!" It grows
(the lie) despite the fact that one is blind
and ignorant—But that is all behind
us now, our nose has shrunk, and we are true
in that we know now what we have to do:
We have to nurture this, our Love, our seed.
My time of month's long-gone and I don't—

Romeo

You're kidding—No, you're serious. I don't
know what to think; I have to think; I won't!
I cannot be a Hamlet-thing; I think
too much (or like the Irish say) I tink.
Tinking is like a chisel and I tick
my Time away in tinking like a mick.
I drink too much; I tink too much; I tock;
I sway as if I were a kind of clock,
a reed; I paint, I draw, I write, I read.
But Doing-Time is here and now I need
to do, ("hacer," in Spanish), duty mad
to do my duty as a doting dad!
I'll go to work wherever work may be.
I'll dig a ditch or I will plant a tree!

Part II

The Nurse (Back in Verona, having received orders from the friar
to go immediately to the two women, who are in a salon getting
their hair done. They jump up, startled, in curlers, when the nurse
arrives…)

O Lady Montague and Capulet!
I know you have been worried but don't fret!
I know you have lost sleep over your bond
of friendship, lest your husbands know, abscond
you need not do; but please to Mantua
come see your new grandchild! I just saw
him for myself! He's healthy and he's calm!
Delivered just this morning in white balm
that comes with birth: protecting him. On dug
of Juliet herself! I see you hug!
You know that all these family quarrels will
be swallowed and forgiven like a pill
that succors, uplifts. This his name will do:
Mercutio Capulet Montague…!!!

Montague (That afternoon, on the outskirts of Verona, at a Club,
getting in an afternoon's worth of pheasant shooting, having
needed to get out of town and "think about things;" although
presently eating peanuts and breaking at the bar… Capulet is also
there.)

O Capulet, you bastard, have you heard?
Your daughter has popped out a little bird.
I heard it through "The Grapevine" from my wife
who's been a member of that Club for life.
You know the way the women gossip, Cap.
I don't know what I'm filled with. Is it sap?
and sentiment. I hear my son now works
in Mantua, a landscaper. He forks
the soil with a hooking thing. With paint
he brushes canvas, in spare time. They're quaint,
these landscapes that he recreates, the trees;
he always loved the sycamores, the seas,
the skies like fields of lavender and suns
like oranges and lemons: fruity ones.

Capulet

Of course I've heard, you heathen; it's a boy.
My wife, as well, is of that vine, deploy
your family, Montague. We'll have a fête
despite that—in agreement—we won't wait
to get along—But they are doing well
Julie, at first, I guess she cooked like hell;
but now she cooks a mean pesto and fish.
My wife, herself, has never cooked a dish;
and though your son has always been a queer,
a weirdo, an eccentric; I don't fear
that he will hurt her any longer. Yes
his paintings are top-notch; they sell, I guess,
which supplements his income potting plants.
It's not a bad life wearing denim pants…

That One Friend

for Stephen Scrafford

The college pell-mell: insane in streetlights:
      I spurned—sequestered; and so did he.
We would sit out on moonlit weeknights
      prone to prattle philosophy...
Minxy gals extolled his features.
      I loafed with him upon the bleachers
in sun at Track Meets where we mused
      on subjects sundry: our legs abused.

We both had smoked from Passion's cigar:
      The college life had chilled our zest.
The embers blackened in our breast
      while we foresaw: The End was not far.
Our wanderlust would soon outrun
      the sober men who boys become.

after Sonnet I. 45 in *Eugene Onegin* by Alexander Pushkin

The Provincial Poet

I am made to live in some calm county.
I relish a rural tranquility.
When all's quiet, I'm rich with a bounty
I must pay for my creativity.
I'm simply entertained, I dabble
farming, gardening. I hear the babble
of flowered streams or of lake-waves lapping
while I'm "Dol-ce far nien-te"* tapping
out on my fingers either warm or cold.
These are blithe hours, happily "squandered."
I sleep a little; I read. I've pondered
how I've given up the pursuit of Gold.
In my leisured prime, have I not tasted
the country's flavor that others wasted?

*An old Italian phrase that literally means "sweet doing nothing" after Sonnet I.
55 of Eugene Onegin by Alexander Pushkin

Grown Ups

When we have summoned up sweet silence,
have balanced an intemperate life;
when we have judged young Passion's violence
absurd and stupid, eschewed strife
which once was welcomed: "Come winds! Come chaos!"
preferring now the placid moss—
Not without disruptive danger—
returning to books like *The Stranger*,
or others which gallop and rage—
we hear the drumbeat pound in the heart;
we play the seasoned soldier's sad part,
who, while trembling, turns the page.
We read of chivalry, of battle,
too old and stiff to mount a saddle.

after Sonnet II. 18 in *Eugene Onegin* by Alexander Pushkin

The Roman Empire Revisited

Our pioneers had felled the forests, burned
the stumps and worked to plough the land with mules.
In those cleared plots the verdant grass that rules
Arcadia had fructified. In turn
sweet-corn would grow. Rocks transformed into walls.
Within those walls they mowed the grain and hay.
They stored the forage for a winter's day
until sly sparks provoked their barns to burn.
So by gradations grew the Empire
till vicious power brought it to its knees:
lured folks to cities, barns consumed in fire,
rock-walls engrossed by pullulating trees…
Necessity was less than our desire
and sunk our cities in the flooding seas.

after Sonnet XXX in Joachim Du Bellay's "The Ruins of Rome"

St. John the Baptist

The last and greatest herald of heaven's King,
adorned in savage skins in deserts wild.
Staunchly he'd take on what the woods could bring;
he found them more harmless than man and mild.

He ate a lot of grasshoppers. He'd fling
dead bark aside while honey-bees were riled.
With sun-burnt body, intense eyes, he'd sing
the psalms of prophets or madmen exiled.

Then he'd burst forth! "All you whose hopes rely
on God, with me, amidst these deserts learn
repentance and from viperous errors turn!"

Who listened to his voice, obeyed his cry?
How many of them, on their way, had went,
while in the caves, his echo roared, "Repent!"

after William Drummond

The Lost Artist

The soul assays a million medicines
        to no avail. I'm lost in antique woods.
I fought and fought entanglement but fins
        of sharks and urban mires have withstood.

I now must live with all of these: My boats
        have flaccid sails. My house hasn't a door.
My mind is like an unhinged monkey's
        who's lost his reason inside a junk drawer.

after a fragment of Michelangelo's

Holy Sonnet 19

O, to challenge me, two selves meet in one:
Inconstancy ironically begets
a constant habit. Like a reed that lets
the wind sway it, willy-nilly, I shun
yesterday's vows; I'm like a hypocrite
who fesses-up, then walks outside to sin.
One half is hot, one half is cold, within
this stubborn mule who loves, then loathes, the bit.
I pray; I'm mute; I'm chaste; I'm lewd; I pine
for Life, not Heaven; but then here today
I see my fatal error and I pray
for all of His forgiveness one more time.
I'm like a fever, and yet I still know,
my best days are when my head is bent low.

after John Donne

The Infinite

These hills are dear to me as they are lonely.
Dear is this hedgerow, which cuts off the view
of the horizon, because here I see
sitting, gazing, with my mind's eye, the true—
the infinite spaces, depthless repose,
till what I feel is nearly fear. The breeze
blowing in these branches, the leafy clothes—
I start to compare—of the rustling trees—
with endless stillness and the setting sun,
eternal peace and the dead season passed,
juxtaposed with the present, lively one,
remind me that mere earthly things don't last.
Thus my mind: in stillness, then noise, goes round,
and flounders sweetly in this sea I've found.

after Giacomo Leopardi

About the Author

Reid McGrath is the winner of the Society of Classical Poet's 2015 Poetry Competition. He also was awarded 2nd Place in Lyric Magazine's 2015 College Competition. He is a poet and writer residing with his wife and childen in Pawling, New York.

www.ingramcontent.com/pod-product-compliance
Lightning Source LLC
Chambersburg PA
CBHW030850090426
42737CB00009B/1172